Hello Kitty
& Her Friends
Crafts Club

Hello Kitty®
Stitch 'n' Sew
Activity Book

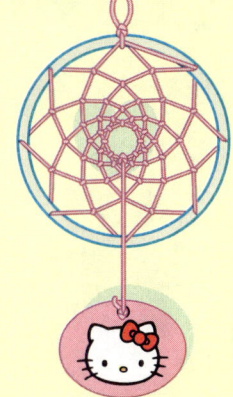

by Kris Hirschmann

Scholastic Inc.

New York Toronto London Auckland Sydney
Mexico City New Delhi Hong Kong Buenos Aires

Designer: Peggy Gardner
Photographs: Kayt Hester-Lent
Illustrations: Yancey Labat

ISBN: 0-439-32847-0

12 11 10 9 8 7 6 5 4 3 2 1   2 3 4 5 6/0

Printed in the U.S.A.
First Scholastic printing, August 2002

Table of Contents

Sewing Is Fun!

String comes in all kinds of great textures—from thread to thick yarn. It also comes in just about every pretty color you can imagine. It's no wonder Hello Kitty loves crafts that use string so much!

In this book, Hello Kitty shares with you 19 of her favorite string projects. To make all these crafts, Hello Kitty has brought along her friends Tim and Tammy to help her out.

You can ask your friends to help you, too, if you want. There's plenty of fun for everyone in this book— no strings attached!

Let's Get Started

With this book, you get five colors of lanyard, six colors of yarn, three colors of string, two embroidery needles, a plastic embroidery mat, measuring tape, and a mini tote bag to store all of your supplies.

Anything else you'll need for these crafts can be found around your house or at a craft store. Ask a grown-up for help if you can't find an item. You'll need:

- Glue
- Craft sticks
- Pencil
- Colored pencils
- Tracing paper

- Scissors
- Drinking straws
- Tape
- Balloon
- Disposable cups

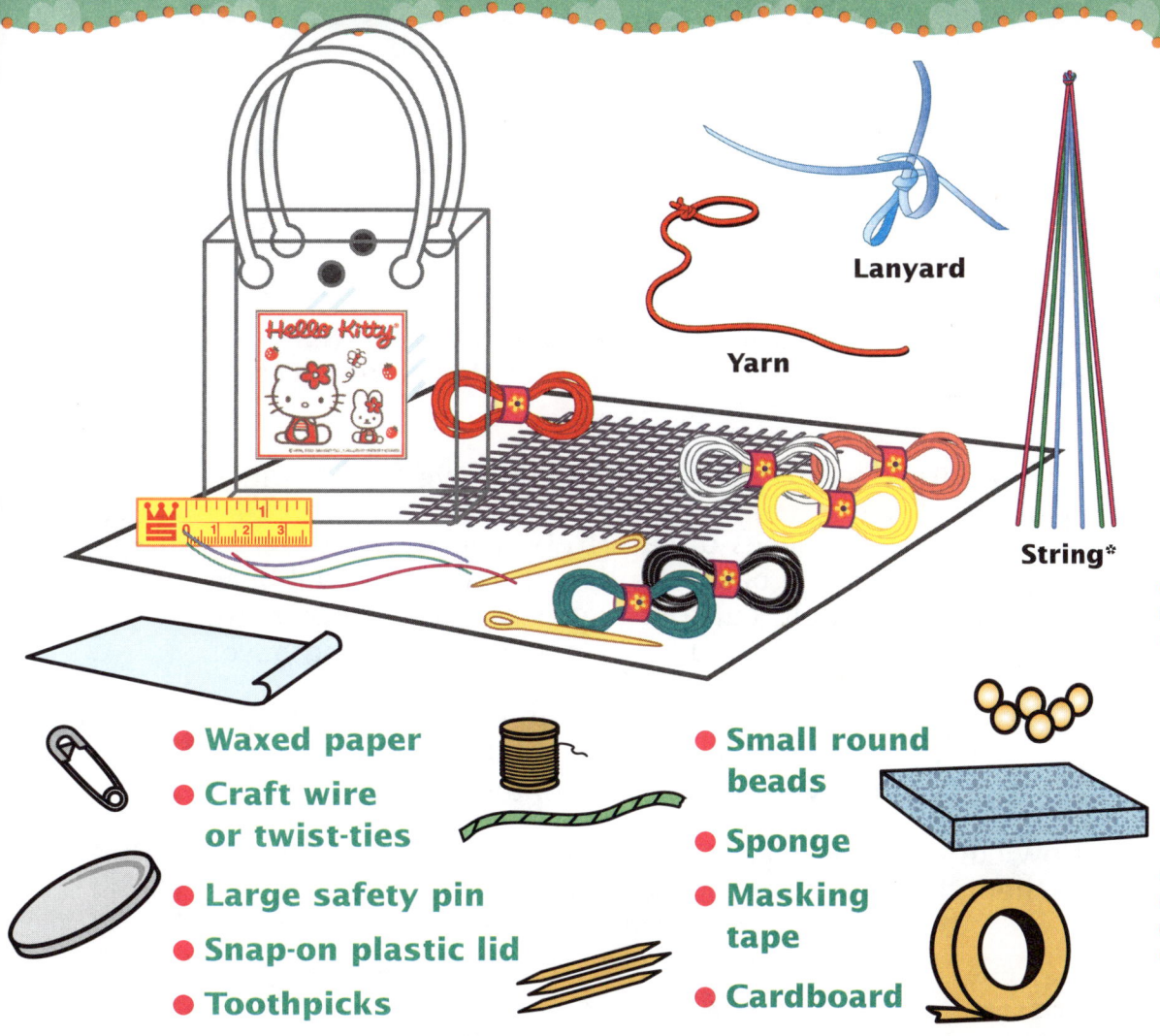

Lanyard

Yarn

String*

- **Waxed paper**
- **Craft wire or twist-ties**
- **Large safety pin**
- **Snap-on plastic lid**
- **Toothpicks**
- **Small round beads**
- **Sponge**
- **Masking tape**
- **Cardboard**

Just in case you run out of materials, you can buy more at any craft store. (*The type of string found in this kit is called "embroidery floss.")

Super String Art

Drinking-straw Loom:

A drinking-straw loom makes it easy to weave artistic belts, funky straps for a Hello Kitty purse, and other long, thin crafts.

What You Do:

1. Cut two drinking straws in half so you have four 4" pieces.

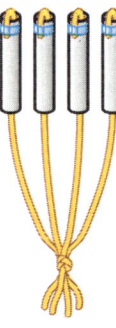

2. Cut four pieces of yarn to be your weaving base. The longer the base, the longer your loom will be. To make a belt, cut four pieces of yarn approximately 3½' long each, and use them as your weaving base.

3. Feed a piece of yarn through each of your straw pieces. Tape each yarn end to the straws, as shown. Tie all four of the other ends of the yarn together in one big knot.

4. Now cut two long pieces of yarn in any colors you like. Hold them together so their ends are even. Tie the strings in a knot around one of the straw pieces near the bottom of the straw. Weave the yarn in and out of the straws you crafted in steps 1–3, as shown.

What You Need:

- Scissors
- 2 eight-inch drinking straws
- Measuring tape
- Yarn (1–4 colors)
- Tape

4

5. Bring the yarn around the fourth straw and then weave it in and out of the straws in the opposite direction. The weaving should be opposite to how you wove in step 4, as shown. When you reach the end of the straws, pull the yarn tightly.

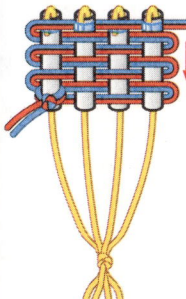

6. Weave your way up the straws, pulling tightly at the end of each row. When you get close to the top of the straws, push your weaving down a couple of inches. The bottom part of the weaving will fall off the straws onto your weaving base.

7. Repeat step 6 until your weaving base is completely covered.

8. Untape the straws and pull them off the weaving base. Tie the ends of the weaving base and the woven yarn ends into one big knot. Tie a knot in the other end as well. (The yellow tassels in the picture are the color used as the weaving base.)

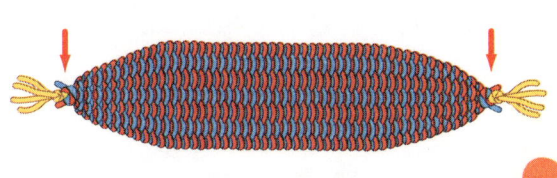

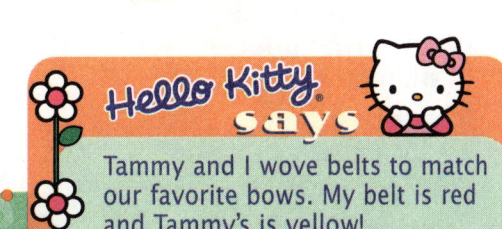

Hello Kitty says

Tammy and I wove belts to match our favorite bows. My belt is red and Tammy's is yellow!

String Geo-art:

You can make lots of neat patterns with this technique, just like Hello Kitty, Tim, and Tammy do.

What You Do:

1. Poke eight toothpicks into the edge of the cardboard circle. Make sure they're arranged evenly in a circle, as shown.

2. Use a double knot to tie one piece of string to any toothpick.

3. Pull the string over one toothpick and under the next one, as shown.

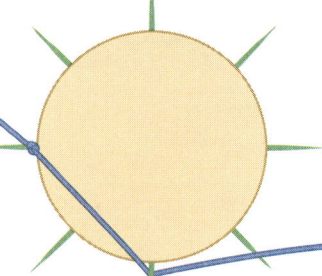

4. Now pull the string over the next two toothpicks in the circle and under the third one, as shown.

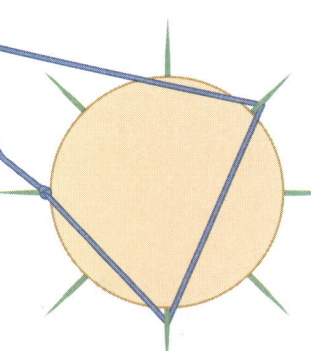

What You Need:

- **8 toothpicks**
- **Circle of corrugated cardboard, about 4" in diameter**
- **Measuring tape**
- **Several feet of string (any color)**
- **Scissors**

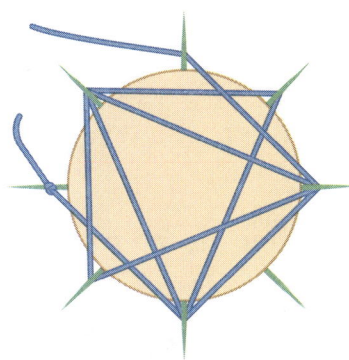

5. Repeat steps 3 and 4 (skipping over one toothpick and then over two) until the design is completed. Watch the pattern to know when you're done. If you start repeating the pattern, you have done too much. HINT: A design always ends on the same toothpick where it started.

6. Tie the ends together in a double knot to secure your design. Then tie another knot with both ends to make a hanging loop. Trim the loose ends.

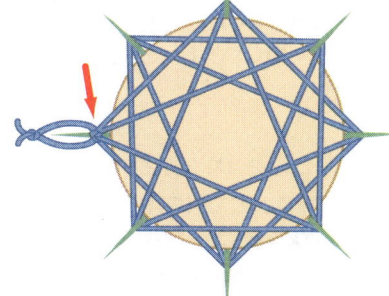

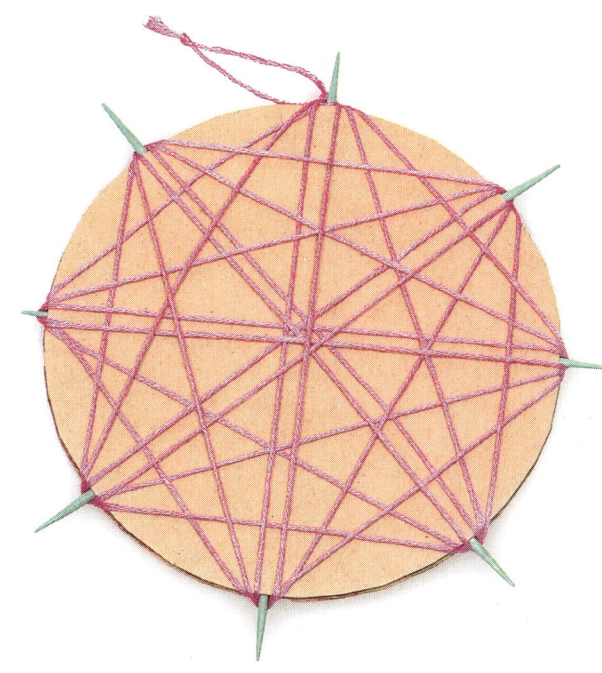

7. Now you have a great work of art. Hang it up anywhere you like and enjoy it.

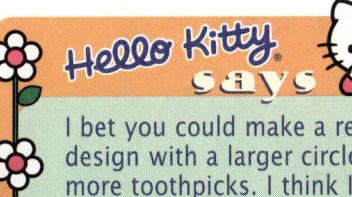

Hello Kitty says

I bet you could make a really BIG design with a larger circle and more toothpicks. I think I'll try it!

Braided Hello Kitty Coasters:

This activity is so simple and fun. All Hello Kitty, Tim, and Tammy do is make an easy braid, then twist it around to make a coaster.

What You Do:

1. Hold the yarn pieces so the ends are even. Then tie all of the ends in a knot. Tape the knot to a table.

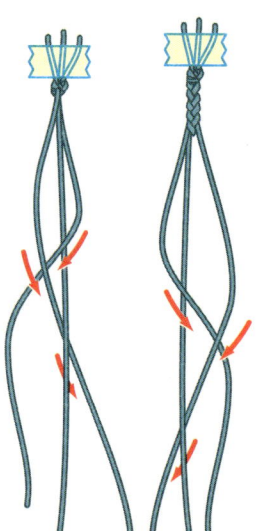

2. Braid the pieces until you reach the end of the strings. Look at the pictures to see how to braid. HINT: Hold the yarn tightly while you braid. You can tape a finished section to the table if you want to shorten your working area.

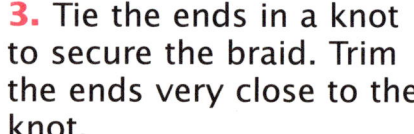

3. Tie the ends in a knot to secure the braid. Trim the ends very close to the knot.

4. Put a blob of glue in the middle of a piece of cardboard (any shape of cardboard is okay, as long as it will be bigger than the size of your coaster). Press the knot of the braid you just made against the glue.

What You Need:

- **3 five-foot pieces of yarn (any colors)**
- **Measuring tape**
- **Tape**
- **Scissors**
- **Glue**
- **Cardboard**

5. Carefully wrap the braid around the knot, as shown, pressing down as you go.

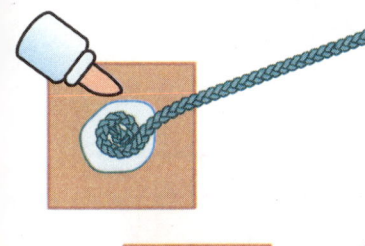

6. When you reach the end of the glued area, run a new line of glue around the outer edge of the braid circle.

7. Keep wrapping the braid around the circle, pressing down as you go.

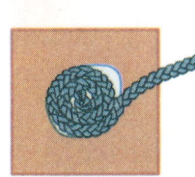

8. Repeat steps 6 and 7 until you reach the end of the braid. Glue down the loose string ends, then set your coaster aside until it dries.

9. Trim away any exposed cardboard to finish your craft.

Hello Kitty **says**

I can't decide which colors to use. This craft is pretty in any color!

Friends Forever

Friendship crafts are the greatest! They're fun to make and fun to give to special friends. Hello Kitty, Tim, and Tammy share their favorite projects with you.

In-a-Twist Bracelet:

This twisting technique lets you make quick and easy bracelets or anklets.

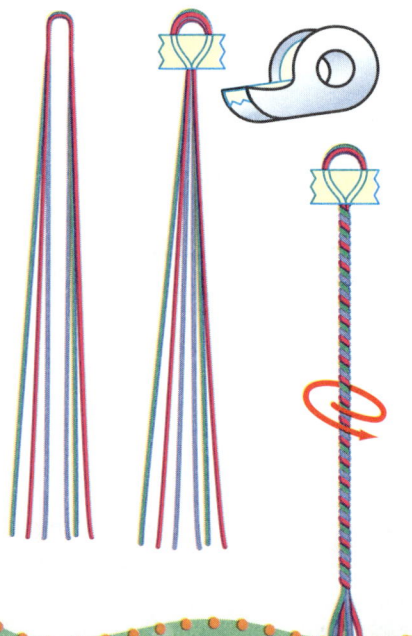

What You Do:

1. Take the three pieces of string and hold them so their ends are even. Then fold them in half. Tape the fold to a table.

2. Twist all the strands of the strings over and over in one direction until they are tightly wound.

What You Need:

- **3 colors of string, 4 feet long each**
- **Measuring tape**
- **Tape**
- **Scissors**

3. Put one finger in the middle of your wound strands and hold the string tightly. Bring the loose ends up to the taped end and press down to hold them all together.

4. Quickly pull your finger out of the bottom fold. All of the strands will twist together.

5. Untape the string and tie all of the strands together in one big knot a few inches below the top fold. Trim the strands low enough to cut through the fold.

6. Pull open a little loop in the folded end, and tie the loose ends through it to wear your friendship craft!

11

Hello Kitty says

This is the best friendship bracelet I ever made. Awesome!

Heart Pendant:

How knotty a knot can you knot? See if you can knot your way to Hello Kitty's heart pendant.

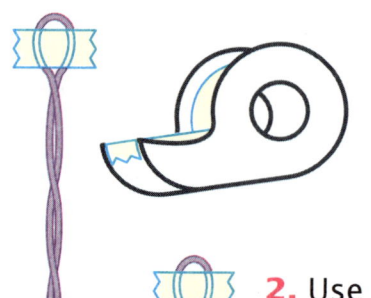

What You Do:

1. Fold the craft wire in half and twist it a little bit to join the two strands. Tape the top loop to a table. HINT: If you don't have craft wire, trim the paper off some twist-ties, and then twist them together until they're 12" long.

2. Use a double knot to tie the string to the wire.

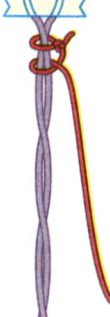

3. Now start your weaving by making knots around your wire or twist-ties, as shown. Pull tightly.

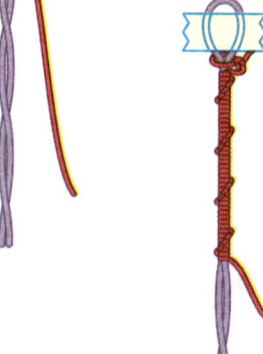

4. Repeat step 3 until you have made about 4" of knots. HINT: The knots will start to twist around the wire. Pull the loose end of the string under the wire when the knots have twisted most of the way around. This will make it easier to work with.

What You Need:

- 12" of craft wire or twist-ties
- Measuring tape
- Tape
- Scissors
- String (any color)

5. Untape the wire. Bend the wire into a heart shape. Tie the string ends in a double knot at the top of the heart shape.

6. Twist the wire ends together several times.

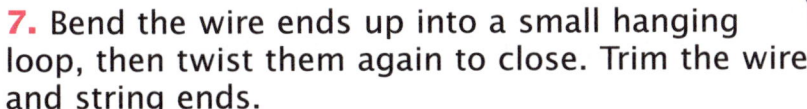

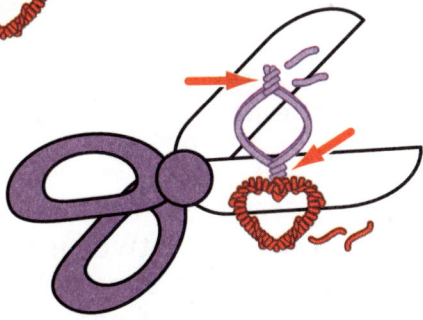

7. Bend the wire ends up into a small hanging loop, then twist them again to close. Trim the wire and string ends.

8. Cut a piece of string long enough to fit around your neck. Feed it through the hanging loop of your heart pendant. Tie the ends together. Now your pendant is ready to wear!

Hello Kitty says

Hearts always make me think of friendship and love. That's why I like them so much!

Lots-of-Knots Friendship Bracelet:

This Hello Kitty bracelet is so neat because it's made with two different patterns.

What You Do:

1. Hold three 4-foot-long strands of string so their ends are even, then fold them in half and tie them in a knot, leaving a small loop at the top. Tape the loop to a table.

2. Arrange the strings so that two strands of the same color are on either edge.

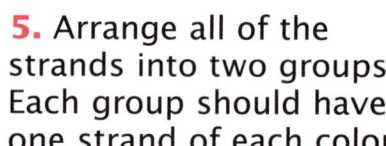

3. To start your first pattern, knot those strands around the other strands, as shown. Pull the knot tightly, making sure it is pushed as far up as it will go.

4. Knot those same strands again, as shown. Be careful! You're knotting a bit differently than in step 3. The strand that was on top last time is now underneath. Keep making these two knots for about ¾".

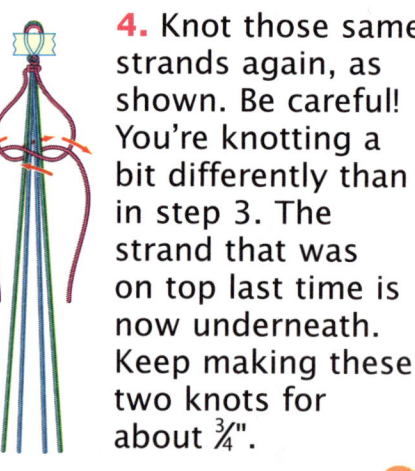

5. Arrange all of the strands into two groups. Each group should have one strand of each color.

What You Need:

- **3 colors of string, 4 feet long each**
- **Measuring tape**
- **Tape**
- **Scissors**

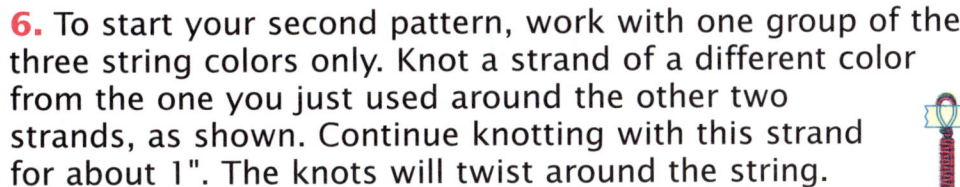

6. To start your second pattern, work with one group of the three string colors only. Knot a strand of a different color from the one you just used around the other two strands, as shown. Continue knotting with this strand for about 1". The knots will twist around the string.

7. Working with the other group of strings, knot a strand of the third color of string around the other two strands, as shown. Continue knotting with this strand for about 1".

8. Repeat steps 2 through 4 using the same color you used to start off the bracelet.

9. Now, repeat steps 5 through 7, always using the long strand to make the knots.

10. Again, repeat steps 2 through 4, using the same color from the beginning and middle of your bracelet.

11. Tie one big knot with all the strands. Trim the loose ends, leaving about 3" below the final knot.

Hello Kitty says

This bracelet takes a while to create because there are so many small stitches to make. But this two-pattern design is worth it!

Hello Kitty Dream Catcher:

If you put this cute Hello Kitty dream catcher above your bed, it will help keep away any bad dreams.

What You Do:

1. Cut a circle out of the middle of a plastic lid, as shown. Then cut eight small notches around the outer rim of the lid (ask a grown-up for help). Space the notches evenly.

2. Tie a small loop in one end of the string.

3. Use a double knot to tie the looped end to any notch on the plastic lid. Then thread the loose end of the string through your embroidery needle.

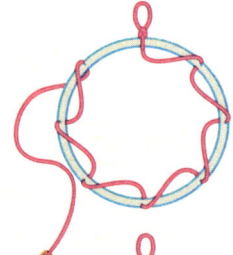

4. Loop the string up and around each notch, as shown. The string should be pulled straight but not too tight.

5. Once you've woven around the circle once, loop the string up and around the center of the next string segment, as shown. Pull the string straight with each stitch.

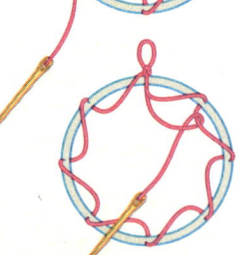

What You Need:

- **Scissors**
- **Snap-on plastic lid (the kind that comes on margarine tubs)**
- **5 feet of string (any color)**
- **Measuring tape**
- **Embroidery needle**
- **Pencil**
- **White tracing paper**
- **Cardboard**
- **Colored pencils**
- **Pin**

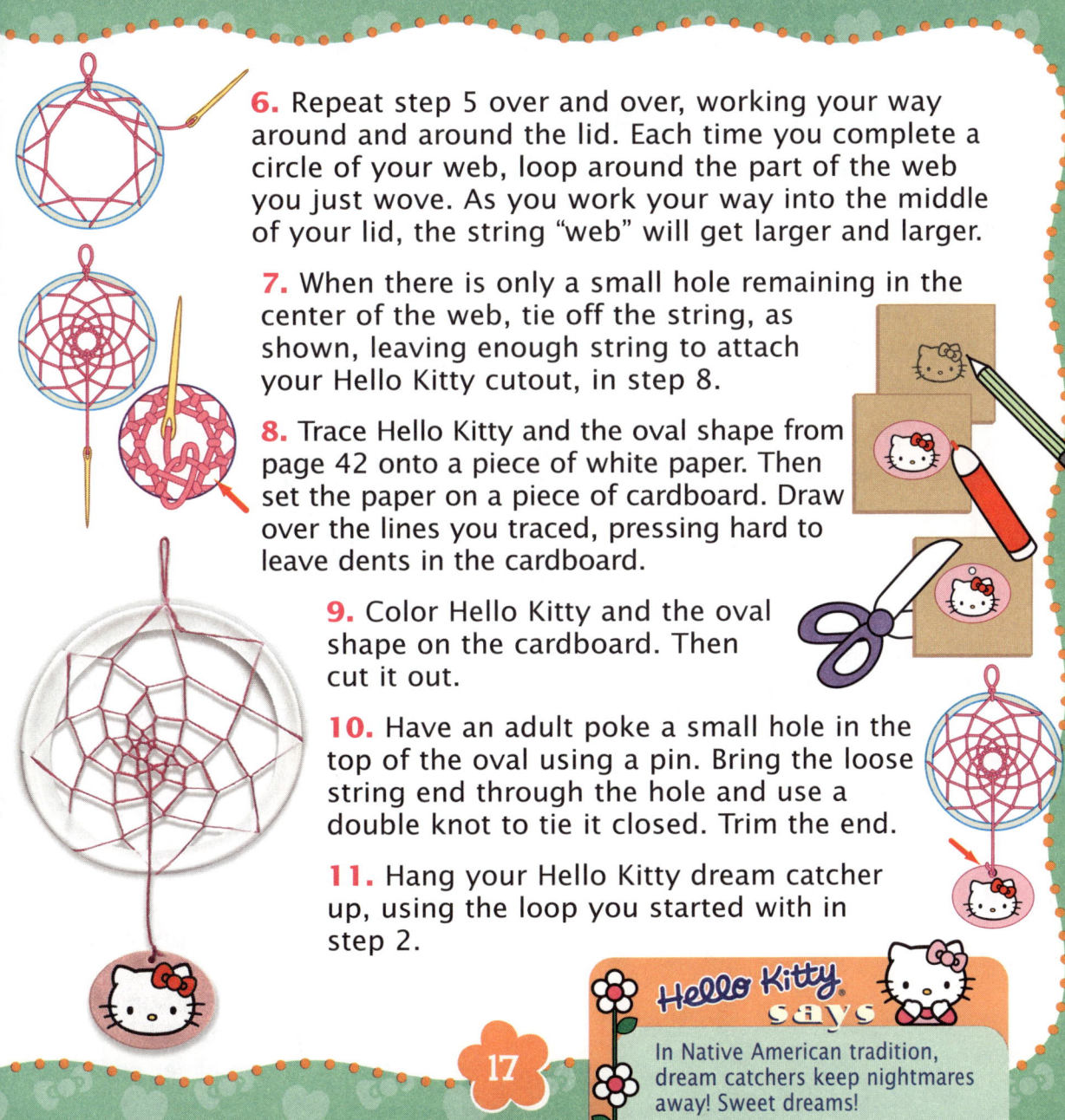

6. Repeat step 5 over and over, working your way around and around the lid. Each time you complete a circle of your web, loop around the part of the web you just wove. As you work your way into the middle of your lid, the string "web" will get larger and larger.

7. When there is only a small hole remaining in the center of the web, tie off the string, as shown, leaving enough string to attach your Hello Kitty cutout, in step 8.

8. Trace Hello Kitty and the oval shape from page 42 onto a piece of white paper. Then set the paper on a piece of cardboard. Draw over the lines you traced, pressing hard to leave dents in the cardboard.

9. Color Hello Kitty and the oval shape on the cardboard. Then cut it out.

10. Have an adult poke a small hole in the top of the oval using a pin. Bring the loose string end through the hole and use a double knot to tie it closed. Trim the end.

11. Hang your Hello Kitty dream catcher up, using the loop you started with in step 2.

Hello Kitty says

In Native American tradition, dream catchers keep nightmares away! Sweet dreams!

Tiny Friendship Dolls:

Whenever Hello Kitty has a worry, she puts one of these little friends near her bed at night. The doll carries her cares away while she sleeps!

What You Do:

1. Cut off one-third of a toothpick. Glue it to the back of the other toothpick to make a cross shape, as shown. Let the glue dry.

2. Hold the strings so their ends are even. Tie the strings together near one of the ends.

3. Feed both strings through a small round bead. This will be your doll's head.

5. Hold one string so it runs straight down the toothpick body of the doll. Wrap the other string around and around the toothpick until you reach the "arms."

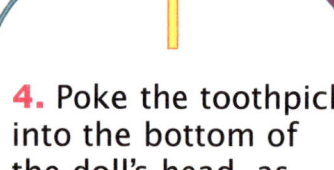

4. Poke the toothpick into the bottom of the doll's head, as shown.

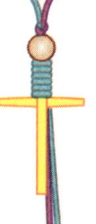

What You Need:

- Scissors
- 2 toothpicks
- Glue
- 2 six-inch pieces of string (any 2 colors)
- Measuring tape
- Small round bead
- Tissue paper or fabric scraps (optional)

6. Now wrap the string around your doll's arm area in a crisscross pattern, as shown.

7. Below the arms, wrap the string a few more times around your doll's body.

8. Now hold the string you've been wrapping with so it runs down the toothpick, and start wrapping with the second color of string to make the bottom part of the doll's clothing. Wrap until you have almost reached the bottom of the toothpick.

9. Glue both strings to the toothpick to finish your friendship doll. When the glue is dry, trim the string ends.

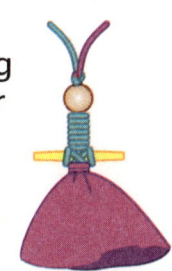

10. You can add a skirt to your doll, using colored tissue paper or scraps of fabric. Wrap string around your doll's waist to hold the skirt in place.

Hello Kitty says

You can never have too many friends...or too many friendship dolls!

Sew Cool!

It's so much fun to needlepoint. There are so many cool things
you can make with a needle and thread or yarn.

How to Needlepoint:

**Three of the crafts in this section use a technique called needlepoint.
Once you've learned these easy steps, you'll whiz through the crafts
that follow!**

Starting the Needlepoint:

Pull the needle through a hole in the mat.
Pull the yarn almost all the way through,
leaving 1" of yarn on the back side of the
mat. Then make a few needlepoint stitches
that loop around the loose end of your yarn
to hold it in place.

Front view

Back view

Needlepoint Stitches:

One needlepoint stitch goes diagonally between two holes,
as shown. Then, the stitch begins again in
the hole below the one you just went
through, as shown here. All of the stitches
should lean in the same direction.

Front view

To Start a New Row:

When you're done stitching one row of one part of the pattern, you need to stitch the row below it. To do this, pull your needle

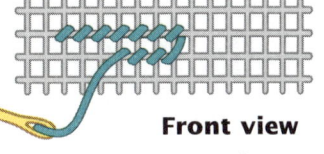

Front view

through the hole that is diagonally below the row you want to stitch. Then pull the needle up into the row you just sewed. You are now following the regular steps for needlepoint stitches, but you're moving in the opposite direction.

To End a Strand:

When you're done stitching in a section of the pattern, pull the yarn to the back and trim off all but 1" of it. Then, when you start a new color, be sure to stitch over this piece of yarn to hold it in place.

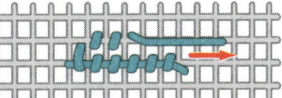

Back view

To Change Colors:

You should complete an entire section of a pattern (like all of Hello Kitty's bow, for example—see pages 22–23) before

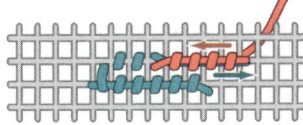

Back view

you begin a new pattern. A new section would mean using a new color. To change colors, end the color you're using first (see To End a Strand) and begin with a new color of string, just as you would if you were starting the needlepoint (see page 20).

To Finish Your Needlepoint:

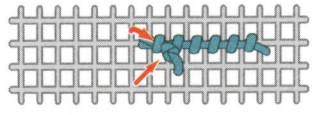

Front view

When you're done with your needlepoint, pull the yarn to the back, then through the last loop you stitched, and tie it in a double knot.

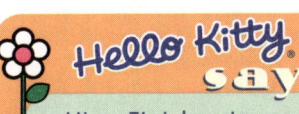

Hello Kitty says

Hint: Finish using one color before starting a new color. After each stitch, pull the yarn until it is firm but not too tight.

Hello Kitty's Needlepoint:

Needlepoint is a traditional craft that is just as much fun today as it ever was. Tim and Tammy made this great needlepoint portrait of Hello Kitty. Now you try it!

What You Do:

1. Cut a piece of your plastic mat that is 24 to 25 holes wide by 21 holes deep. IMPORTANT: The holes in the mat are rectangular, not square. Make sure the narrow edges of the holes are pointing up and down, as shown, when you measure your mat.

2. Trace the Hello Kitty pattern on page 43 lightly onto one side of the mat with a pencil. Use your white yarn to begin the pattern and, following the basic needlepoint instructions on pages 20–21, stitch in the pattern for Hello Kitty.

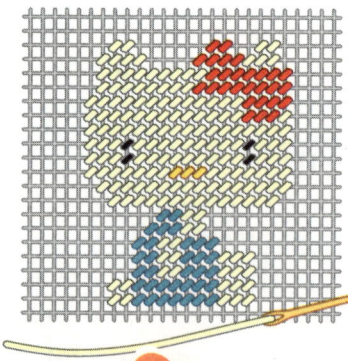

3. Switch colors and stitch in Hello Kitty's clothes and bow.

What You Need:

- Scissors
- Plastic mat
- Pencil
- 6 colors of yarn, various lengths
- Embroidery needle
- Measuring tape

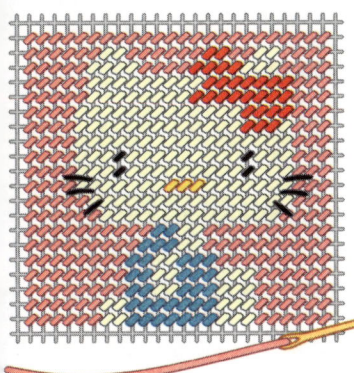

4. Needlepoint a background all around Hello Kitty in whatever color you like.

5. Sew Hello Kitty's whiskers and eyes over the background pattern.

6. Using a 6-foot piece of yarn (yellow in the picture), sew buttonhole stitches all the way around the outside of the mat. Look at the picture to see how.

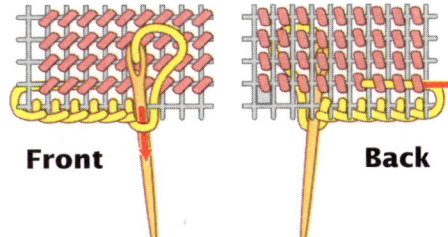

Front   **Back**

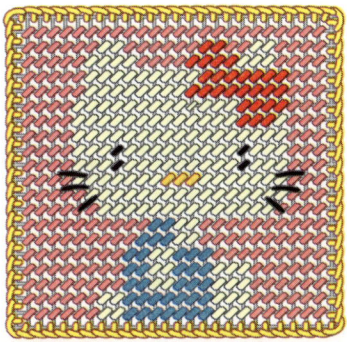

Hello Kitty says

Wow! It's a picture of me! Thanks, Tim and Tammy!

Hello Kitty's Cross-stitch:

Hello Kitty loves to cross-stitch portraits of her friends. Here she makes a picture of Tammy.

What You Do:

1. Cut a piece of plastic mat that is 18 holes wide by 16 holes deep. IMPORTANT: The holes in the mat are rectangular, not square. Make sure the narrow edges of the holes are pointing up and down, as shown, when you measure your mat.

2. Trace the pattern on page 42 onto the mat, then cross-stitch Tammy's face and bow. Follow the basic needlepoint instructions (on pages 20–21), but, when you finish stitching a row, don't start a new one. Instead, stitch back over the row with the stitches leaning in the opposite direction, as shown below.

Basic needlepoint stitch

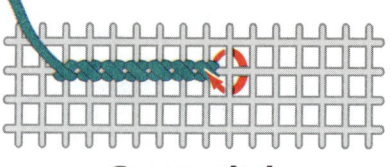

Cross-stitch

What You Need:

- **Scissors**
- **Plastic mat**
- **Pencil**
- **Embroidery needle**
- **6 colors of yarn, various lengths**
- **Measuring tape**

24

Detail of Tammy's nose

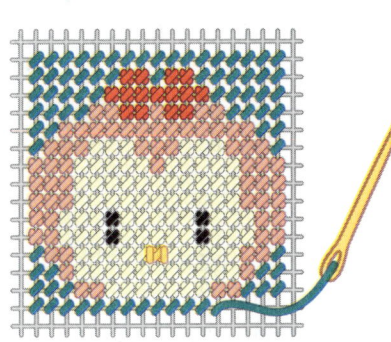

3. Make a couple of up-and-down stitches, as shown, to widen Tammy's nose.

4. Use a single strand of yarn to needlepoint a background all around Tammy.

5. Using a 4-foot piece of yarn, sew buttonhole stitches all the way around the outside of the mat. Look at the picture to see how.

Front   **Back**

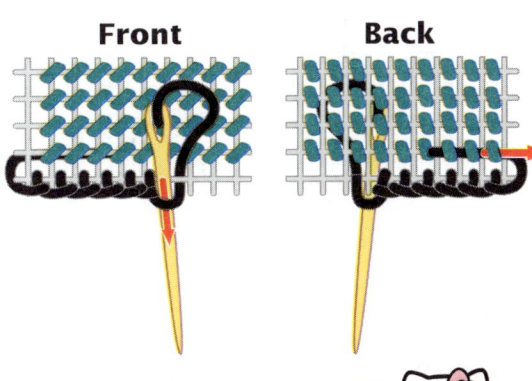

I bet this cross-stitch picture would look great in a frame. What do you think?

Monogram Patches:

Use an easy chain-stitch technique to make these fun monogram patches. Hello Kitty pinned one to her jacket, Tim glued one to his backpack, and Tammy taped one to her locker!

What You Do:

1. Cut a piece of plastic mat. It should be about 8 holes wide by 8 holes deep, if you want to sew a single letter, and 10 holes wide by 8 holes deep, if you want to sew two letters. Here, we're sewing Hello Kitty's initials. Sketch the initials on the mat with your pencil to use as an outline when stitching. (See the pattern on page 42 if you'd like to do Hello Kitty's initials.)

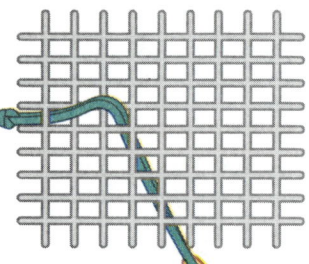

2. Cut a 2-foot piece of yarn. Thread it through the needle and pull until both ends are even. Tie the two ends together in a knot.

3. To make a chain stitch, first poke the needle up through a hole. Pull until the knot reaches the mat. Then skip one hole and poke the needle down through the next hole, as shown.

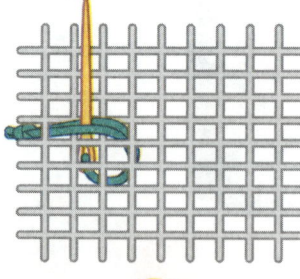

4. Poke the needle up through the hole you skipped and between the two strands of yarn. Pull it tightly.

What You Need:

- Scissors
- Plastic mat
- Pencil
- Measuring tape
- Yarn (any 2 colors)
- Embroidery needle

26

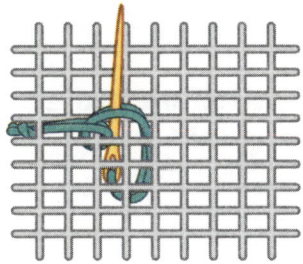

5. Poke the needle down through the next empty hole, then back up through the previous hole, as shown. Repeat as needed to create your letters.

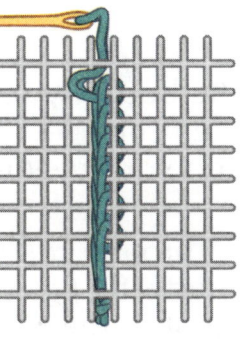

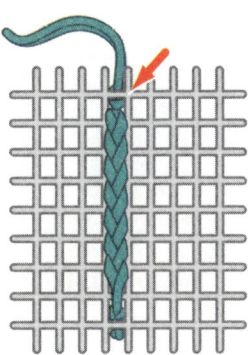

6. To end a row, poke the needle down through the last hole of the row, as shown. Tie off on the back side of the mat, if you're finished, or move on to another row if you're not.

7. When your monogram is done, use a single strand of yarn to fill in the background with needlepoint stitches. (See "How to Needlepoint" on pages 20–21.)

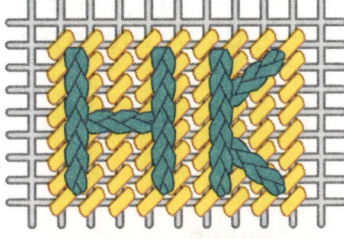

Hello Kitty says

What are your initials? Can you make your own cool monogram name patch?

Sponge Art:

A dry sponge makes a super canvas for an artistic stitching project. Tammy stitched a butterfly on her sponge. Now she wants to show you how to do it, too!

What You Do:

1. Trace the butterfly pattern on page 42 onto one side of a sponge. Cut a 15" piece of red yarn. Thread one end through your needle. Tie a knot in the other end.

2. Push the needle through the sponge along the outline of the butterfly pattern. Pull it through until the knot in the yarn reaches the sponge. Then push the needle back through the sponge in the opposite direction to make a stitch. The stitch should be about ¼" long.

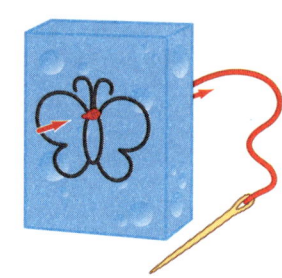

3. Continue making stitches, following the butterfly outline as you go. When you have finished, tie off the string as shown. (HINT: Make sure all the loose ends of the string are on the same side of the sponge.)

What You Need:

- Pencil
- Dry, clean sponge
- Scissors
- Measuring tape
- Red, yellow, and black yarn
- Embroidery needle

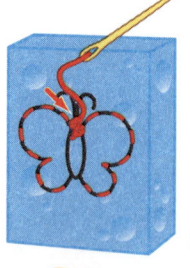

Back

Front

4. Cut an 8" piece of black yarn. Use it to stitch the butterfly's body, head, and antennae using the same technique you followed in steps 1, 2, and 3.

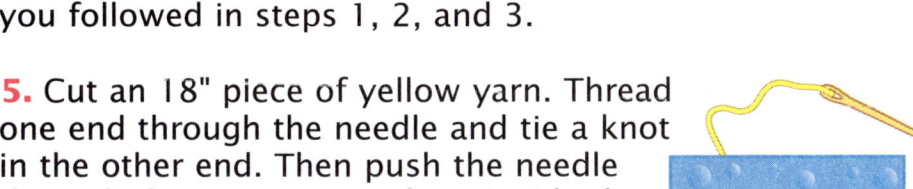

5. Cut an 18" piece of yellow yarn. Thread one end through the needle and tie a knot in the other end. Then push the needle through the sponge anywhere inside the butterfly wing outline. Pull the thread through until the knot in the yarn reaches the sponge.

Side

6. Wrap the yarn twice around the needle, as shown.

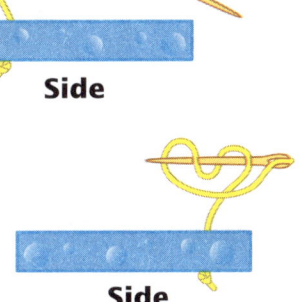

Side

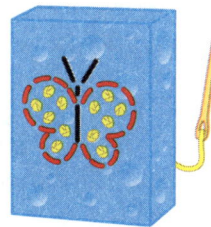

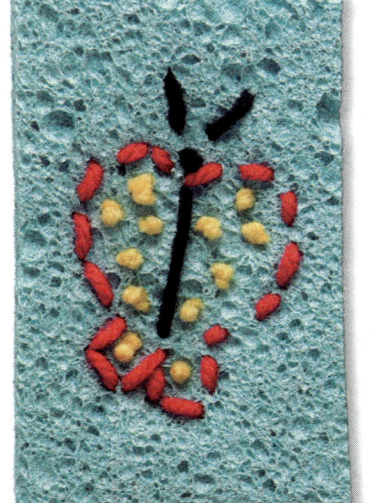

7. Press the wrapped yarn against the sponge to hold it in place, then pull the needle through to make a knot. Pull tight and trim the yarn end.

8. Make as many yellow knots as you like to finish your craft. This will make a pretty pattern on your butterfly's wings!

Hello Kitty says

Who would have thought you could have so much fun with a sponge!

Fun String Things

This section includes some "just for fun" string projects.
Get a group of friends together and try them all!

Little Critter Hammock:

**Hello Kitty loves to laze in a hammock on a hot summer day.
You can make a tiny hammock for your favorite small plush animal!**

What You Do:

1. Cut two pieces of plastic mat that are eight holes wide by one hole deep.

2. Hold the eight yarn pieces so their ends are even. Then tie all of the ends together in one big knot, leaving about 2" of loose string above the knot.

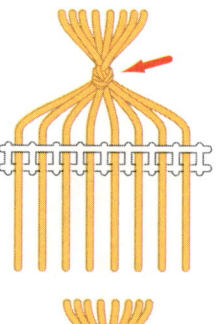

3. Feed a yarn strand through each of the eight holes of one of the mat pieces.

4. Tie the first two strands in a square knot, as shown, leaving about ½" above the knot.

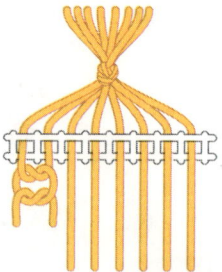

What You Need:

- **Scissors**
- **Plastic mat**
- **8 twelve-inch pieces of yarn (any color)**
- **Measuring tape**

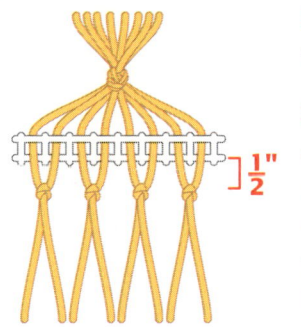

5. Repeat step 4 with the second two strands, then the third, and then the fourth.

6. Pull the first strand away from the others, as shown. Tie the next two strands in a square knot (as you did in step 5), then the next two, and then the next two. You will have one strand left over when you finish this row.

7. Repeat steps 4 through 6 until the loose ends of the string are about 5" long.

8. Repeat steps 4 and 5.

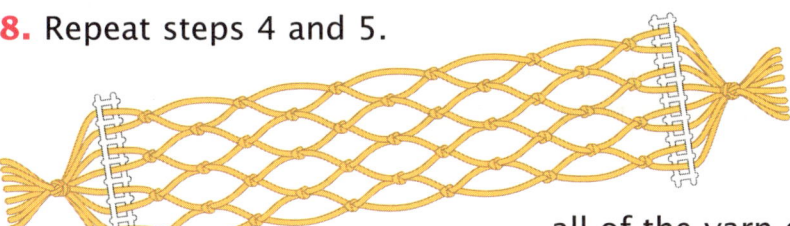

9. Feed each yarn strand through one hole of the second mat piece. Then tie all of the yarn ends in one big knot. Trim the ends, leaving about 2" loose. Hang your hammock wherever you like!

Hello Kitty says

I tied the ends of my little hammock to two candlesticks to hang it. Try it yourself!

Tiny Tassels:

Hello Kitty adds these cute tassels to her birthday gifts to Tim and Tammy for a special homemade touch.

What You Do:

1. Cut six 6" pieces of string. Hold the strings so their ends are even. Then tie one big knot with all the ends, leaving about 2" of string above the knot.

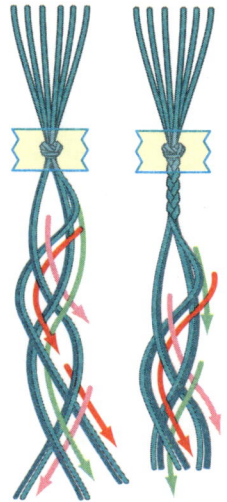

2. Tape the knot to a table so you can work more easily. Then separate the strings into three groups with two strands each. Braid the strands for about 2".

3. Tie a big knot with all the strands at the bottom of the braided section.

4. Find a hard object that is about 1" to 2" wide. (Some rulers are the right width. You could also use a deck of cards or anything else that is about the right width.) Wrap a long piece of string around the object about 20 times.

What You Need:

- Scissors
- Measuring tape
- String (any color)
- Tape
- Hard object (see instructions)

5. Snip through one side of the strings, as shown.

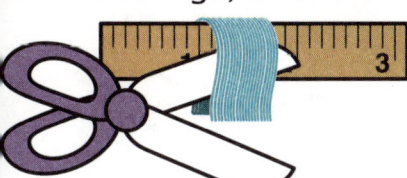

6. Lay the strings flat on a table and spread them out. Set the braided section on top of the strings, with the bottom knot a little below the middle of the strings.

7. Gather the strings around the knot. Tie a piece of string tightly above the knot, as shown.

8. Bend the top string ends down. Tie another piece of string tightly below the knot, as shown.

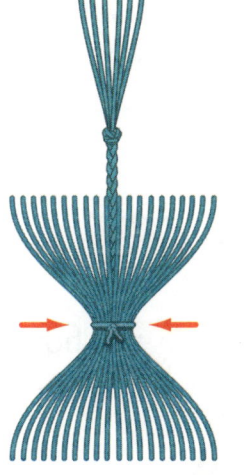

9. Trim the ends of your tassel.

Hello Kitty says

I like to tie tassels to things, like gifts, key chains, or my backpack!

Quick Crochet Bookmark:

It's no fun to lose your place in a book. With this cute Hello Kitty bookmark, you'll always find your place.

What You Do:

1. Hold the two yarn pieces so their ends are even. Then use a double knot to tie the pieces around a pencil, as shown.

2. Loop the yarn pieces around the pencil once.

3. Pull the bottom loop out a little bit. Then pull it up and over the pencil tip. (Make sure it also goes over the top loop.)

4. Repeat steps 2 and 3 until you have worked about 6".

5. Pull the pencil out of the loops. Then feed both yarn ends through the last loop, as shown. Pull it tightly.

6. Trim the top ends. Then tie the bottom ends in a bow to finish your bookmark.

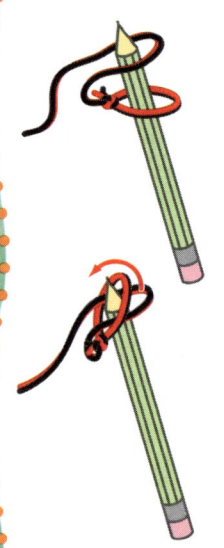

What You Need:

- 2 three-foot pieces of yarn (any colors)
- Measuring tape
- Pencil
- Scissors

Hello Kitty's Balloon Wrap:

This hollow string ball stands up all by itself. You can use your ball as a wind catcher, as an ornament, or as anything else you like.

What You Do:

1. Blow up a balloon until it is about 5" or 6" across. Tie the end closed.

2. Put some glue into a disposable cup.

3. Dunk a piece of yarn in the glue until it's sticky all over. Then wrap the yarn around the balloon in any pattern you like.

4. Repeat step 3 with the other pieces of yarn. Set the string-wrapped balloon on a piece of waxed paper to dry.

5. When the glue is completely dry, use your scissors to pop the balloon. Remove the broken balloon carefully and throw it away. The yarn will hold the balloon's shape!

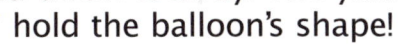

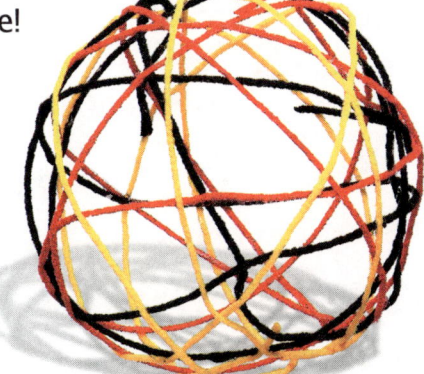

What You Need:

- Balloon
- Measuring tape
- Glue
- Disposable cup
- 3 colors of yarn, 6 feet long each
- Waxed paper
- Scissors

35

Lots of Lanyard

Lanyard crafts are so much fun, and, because lanyard's waterproof, you can wear these crafts all the time—even in the pool!

Square Weave Key Chain:

This basic lanyard craft is so much fun to make that Hello Kitty wants to show you how!

What You Do:

1. Hold the lanyard strands so the ends are even, then fold them in half. Tie all the strands in a knot, leaving a small loop at the top.

2. Hold the loop upside down so the four strands arch outward, as shown.

 **3.** Arrange two of the strands, as shown.

4. Bring the other two strands over, then under the folded strands, as shown.

What You Need:

- **2 pieces of lanyard (3 feet long each)**
- **Measuring tape**
- **Scissors**
- **Key clip or key chain**

5. Pull the strands tightly to create a square base.

6. Repeat steps 3 through 5 until there are about 2" of loose lace remaining.

7. Using a double knot, tightly tie two strands from opposite corners together.

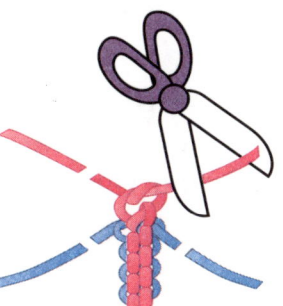

8. Using a double knot, tightly tie the other two strands. Trim the ends.

9. Add a key clip to the looped end or attach to a key chain.

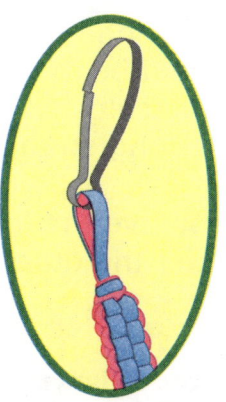

Hello Kitty says

This key chain is great! Now I have a colorful place to hang my keys!

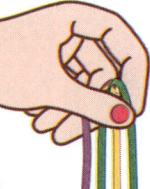

Funky Flat Bracelet:

This bracelet is made using a back-and-forth weaving technique. This is one of Hello Kitty's favorites!

What You Do:

1. Fold one strand of the three-foot lanyard in half. Line up the ends of the other two strands (1 three-foot, 1 one-foot) with the fold.

2. Tie a knot with all the strands and the folded piece, leaving a small loop above the knot. Tape the loop to a table so you can work more easily.

3. Arrange the strands, as shown. The short one should be in the middle. The two strands of the same color go on both sides of the short strand. The long strand should be held out to the side.

4. Weave the long strand under, then over, then under the other three strands, as shown. (Make sure to hold all of the strands flat as you weave.) Pull the lanyard tightly.

What You Need:

- **2 pieces of lanyard (3 feet long each)**
- **1 one-foot piece of lanyard lace**
- **Measuring tape**
- **Tape**
- **Scissors**

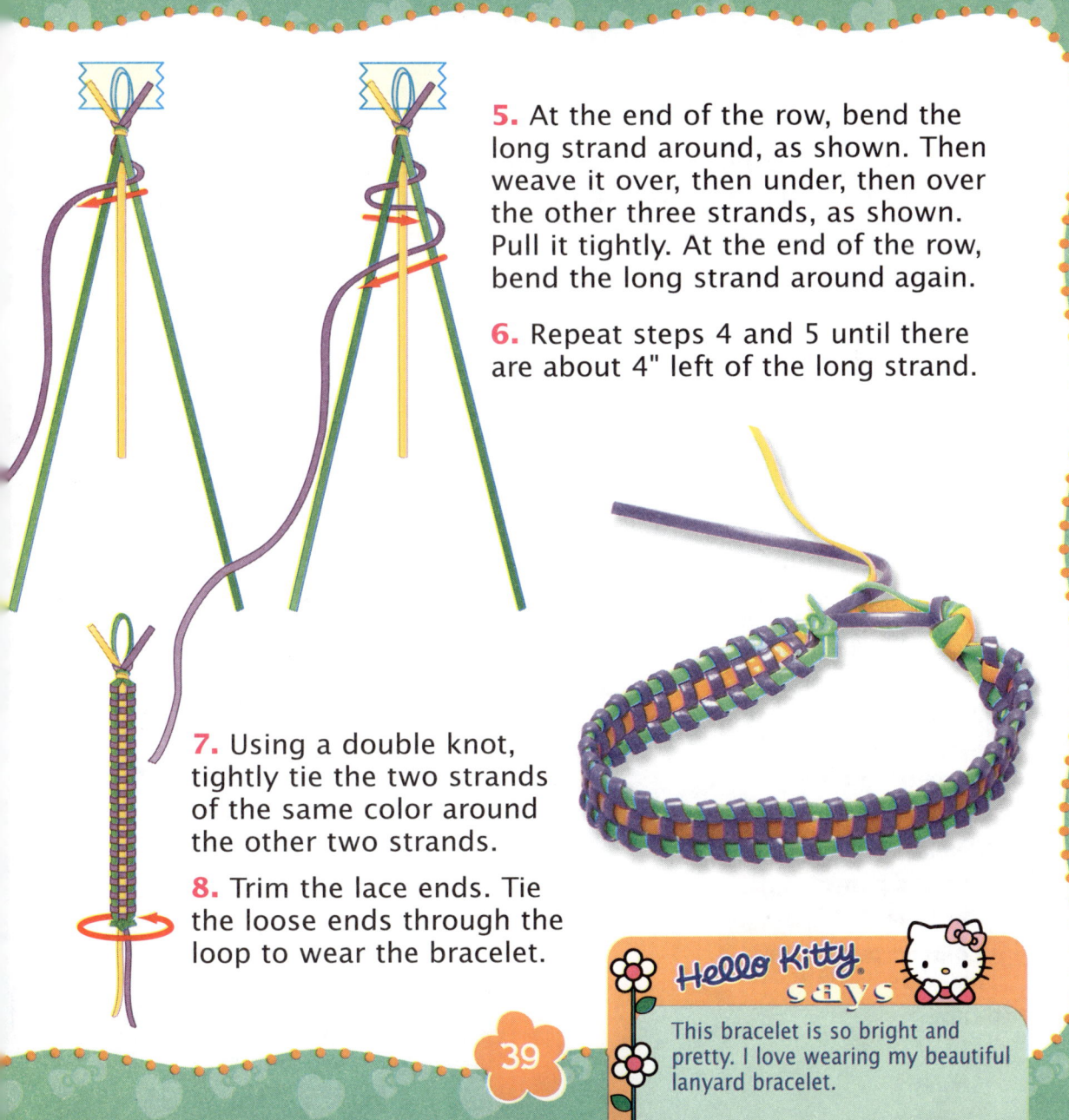

5. At the end of the row, bend the long strand around, as shown. Then weave it over, then under, then over the other three strands, as shown. Pull it tightly. At the end of the row, bend the long strand around again.

6. Repeat steps 4 and 5 until there are about 4" left of the long strand.

7. Using a double knot, tightly tie the two strands of the same color around the other two strands.

8. Trim the lace ends. Tie the loose ends through the loop to wear the bracelet.

Hello Kitty **says**

This bracelet is so bright and pretty. I love wearing my beautiful lanyard bracelet.

Round Weave Pendant:

This pendant is little, but challenging to make. Follow the steps carefully and you'll do fine. Hello Kitty did it and so can you!

What You Do:

1. Hold the lanyard strands so their ends are even, then fold the strands in half.

2. Follow steps 2–5 on pages 36–37 to begin making your pendant.

3. Now you're going to make round stitches to weave your pendant. Follow the pictures to see how to so this. Instead of looping the strands straight across, you'll be looping them *diagonally* across. Continue weaving for about 1".

What You Need:

- **2 one-foot pieces of lanyard (any color)**
- **Measuring tape**
- **Scissors**
- **Pencil**
- **Tracing paper**
- **Cardboard**
- **Colored pencils or markers**
- **Tape**
- **Glue**
- **String**

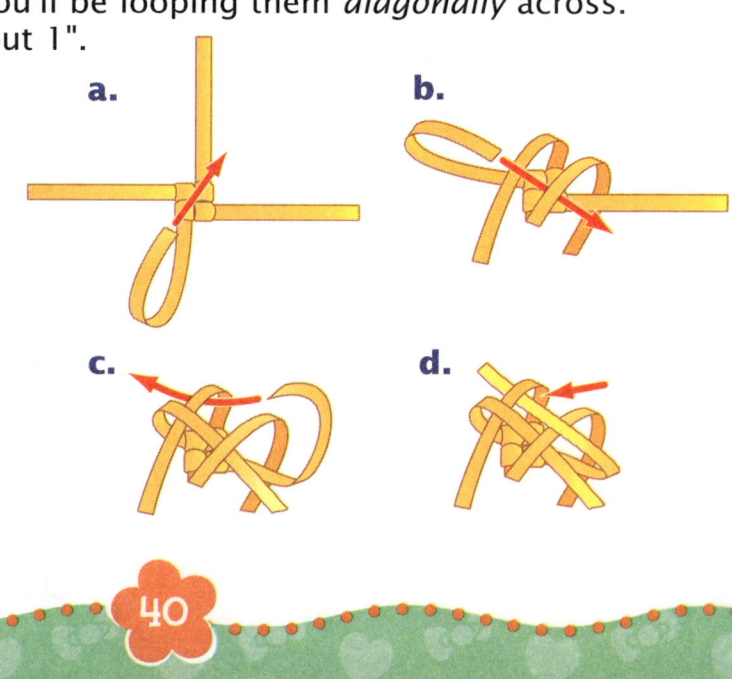

a.

b.

c.

d.

4. Using a double knot, tightly tie two strands from opposite corners together.

5. Using a double knot, tightly tie the other two strands. Trim the ends so that they are 1" long.

6. Trace Tammy's head (see page 43) onto two pieces of cardboard, color them, and cut them out.

7. Now, tape the four strands of lanyard to the back of Tammy's head. Put a drop of glue on top of the tape and glue the second head on top of the first, sandwiching the strands between them.

8. Feed a piece of string through the top loops that is long enough to fit around your head. Tie it in a knot, then wear your round weave pendant as a good luck necklace!

Hello Kitty says

What a pretty necklace! Why not make one with a picture of Tim?

Shapes & Patterns

"Hello Kitty
Dream Catcher,"
pages 16–17

"Monogram Patches," pages 26–27

"Sponge Art," pages 28–29

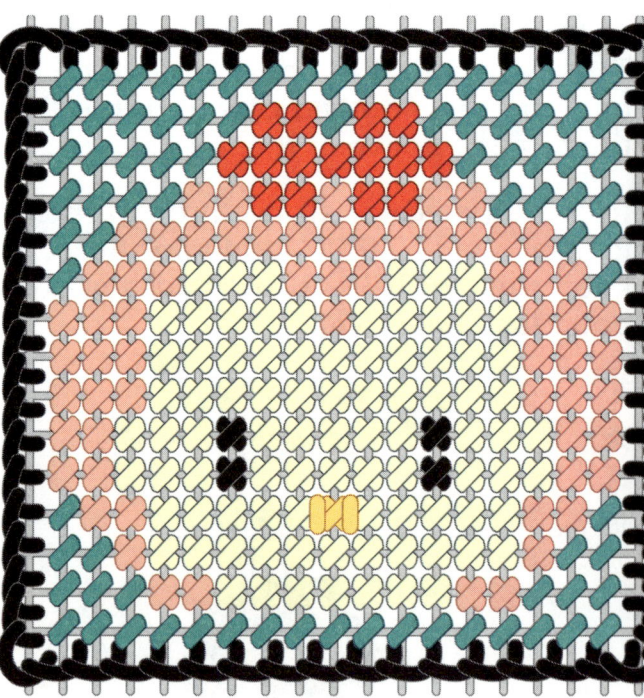

"Hello Kitty's Cross-stitch,"
pages 24–25

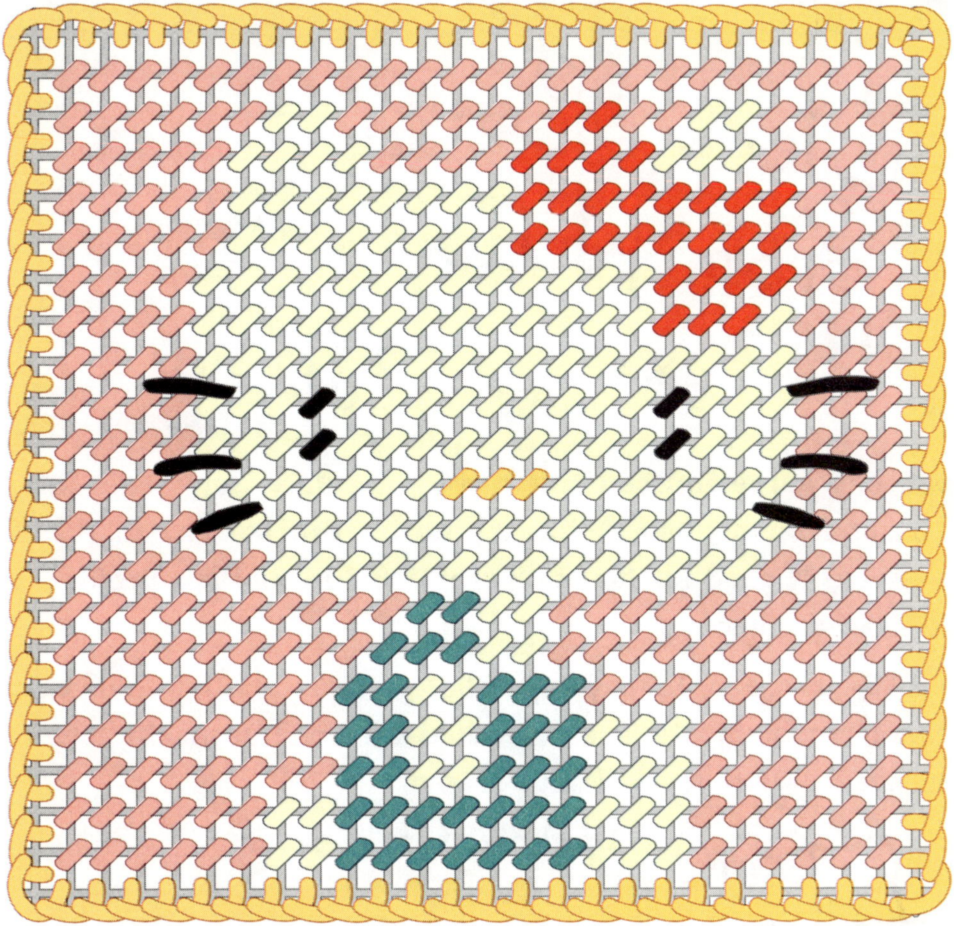

"Hello Kitty's Needlepoint," pages 22–23

"Round Weave Pendant," pages 40–41

43

Sew Long
from Hello Kitty,
Tim, and Tammy

Now that you've finished this book, you can see why Hello Kitty, Tim, and Tammy love string and sewing crafts so much! A little bit of string is good for hours of crafting fun, and the project possibilities are endless.

Hello Kitty, Tim, and Tammy hope that you liked doing all of their favorite string projects. They sure had a lot of fun sharing their special crafts with you and your friends.

Until next time, "Sew Long!"

Love, xoxox
Hello Kitty,
Tim, and Tammy